SUPER SPORTS STAR

LATRELL SPREWELL

Michael J. Pellowski

Enslow Publishers, Inc.

40 Industrial Road	PO Box 38
Box 398	Aldershot
Berkeley Heights, NJ 07922	Hants GU12 6BP
USA	UK

http://www.enslow.com

Dedicated to George Dumas and Jimmy Graves.

Library of Congress Cataloging-in-Publication Data

Pellowski, Michael J.
     Super sports star Latrell Sprewell / Michael J. Pellowski.
          p. cm. - (Super sports star)
     Includes bibliographical references (p.) and index.
     Summary: Examines the personal life, college years, and professional
     career of NBA basketball star Latrell Sprewell, who now plays for the
     New York Knicks.
     ISBN 0-7660-1811-3
     1. Sprewell, Latrell-Juvenile literature. 2. Basketball players-United States-
Biography-Juvenile literature. [1. Sprewell, Latrell. 2. Basketball players. 3. African
Americans-Biography.] I. Title. II. Series.
     GV884.S59 P45 2002
     796.323'092-dc21

                                                                    2001003140

Printed in the United States of America

10 9 8 7 6 5 4 3 2 1

To Our Readers:
We have done our best to make sure all Internet addresses in this book were active and appropriate when we went to press. However, the author and the publisher have no control over and assume no liability for the material available on those Internet sites or on other Web sites they may link to. Any comments or suggestions can be sent by e-mail to comments@enslow.com or to the address on the back cover.

Photo Credits: NBA Entertainment. Photo by Andrew D. Bernstein, p. 42; NBA Entertainment. Photo by Nathaniel S. Butler, pp. 16, 27, 32, 43; NBA Entertainment. Photo by Lou Capozzola, p. 6; NBA Entertainment. Photo by Chris Covatta, p. 23; NBA Entertainment. Photo by Gary Dineen, p. 1; NBA Entertainment. Photo by Garrett Ellwood, pp. 11, 36, 38; NBA Entertainment. Photo by Sam Forencich, pp. 9, 20, 34; NBA Entertainment. Photo by Glenn James, p. 4; NBA Entertainment. Photo by Frank McGrath, p. 29; NBA Entertainment. Photo by Fernando Medina, pp. 18, 24; NBA Entertainment. Photo by Norm Perdue, p. 40; NBA Entertainment. Photo by Rocky Widner, p. 14.

Cover Photo: NBA Entertainment. Photo by Gary Dineen.

CONTENTS

Introduction

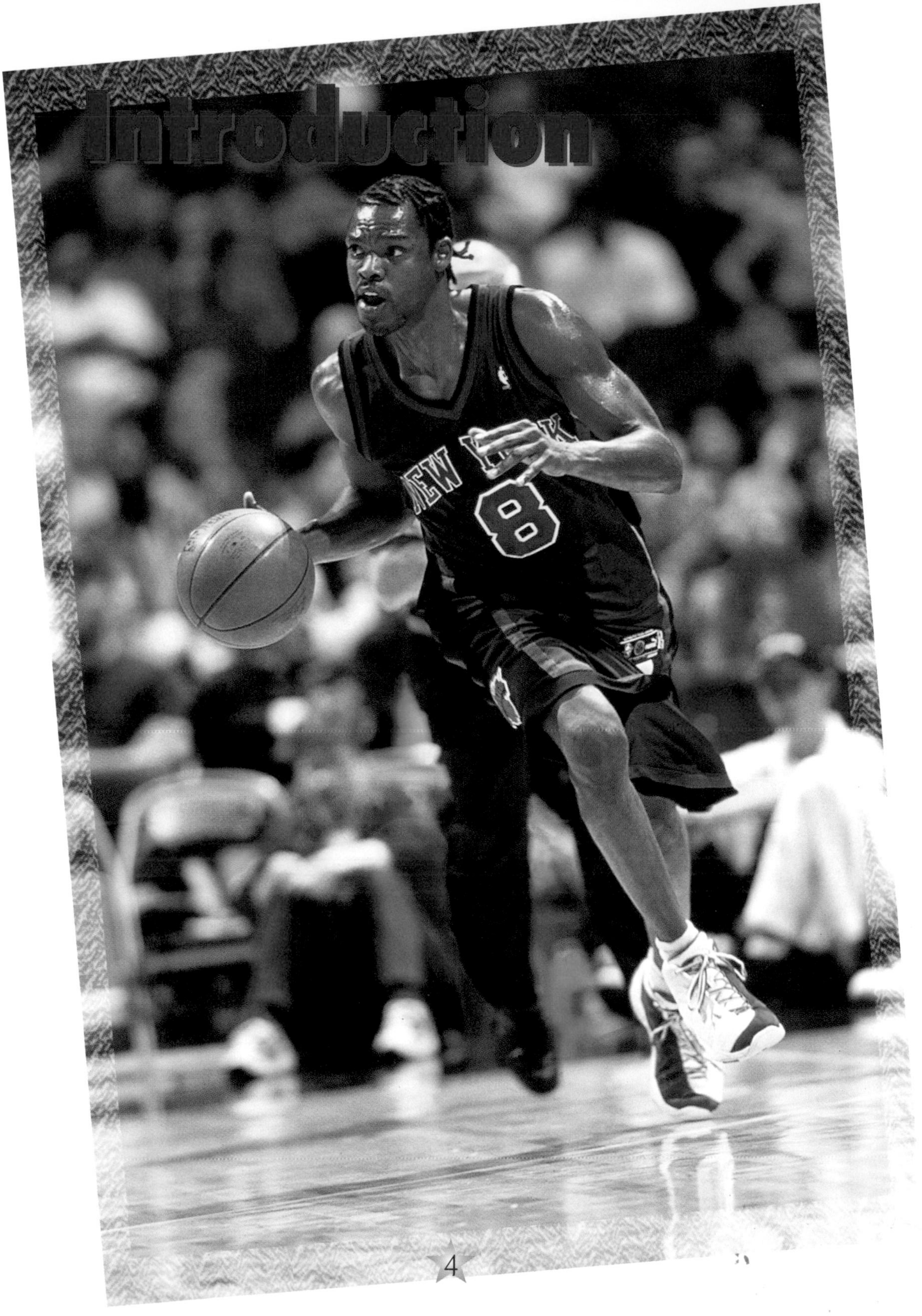

Latrell Sprewell plays guard and forward for the New York Knicks of the National Basketball Association (NBA). He is not the biggest player in the NBA. He is also not the strongest or the fastest player. He is six feet five inches tall and weighs 190 pounds. He wears No. 8 for the Knicks, and he has overcome many obstacles to become one of New York's most popular players.

Fans love watching Sprewell play on both offense and defense. Teammates and opponents both look up to the way he takes charge on the court. His athletic abilities and his energetic style of play are also fun to watch.

Sprewell is best known for his talents on offense. He can drive to the basket, hit the jumper or shoot three-pointers.

He is also known for his defense. He usually leads his team in steals and is also a solid rebounder. Latrell Sprewell can do many things well on the basketball court. Exciting things happen when he is in the game.

Always a Champion

At one time, some NBA coaches, fans, and officials thought Latrell Sprewell had a bad attitude. Now, they are giving Sprewell credit. He has faced his problems and has gotten past them. Today he shows his worth on the basketball court.

Mario Elie of the San Antonio Spurs says Sprewell is a "fiery type of guy. He hits big shots. He's got a warrior's heart."

Latrell Sprewell proved himself during the 1999 NBA Finals against the San Antonio Spurs. He became a key player in the fifth game of the series. The Spurs were ahead in the series, leading the Knicks three games to one. One more win would bring San Antonio the championship.

Time was running out in the game. New York was losing, 78–77. There were only 21 seconds left on the clock. The Knicks had the ball out of bounds. If they did not score right away, San Antonio would win the championship.

Who did the Knicks turn to for help? Who did they count on to take that important shot? They hoped Latrell Sprewell would win the game.

Sprewell is known as "Spree" to his teammates. He was playing his first season for the Knicks. But New York felt sure that Sprewell could help them win.

Sprewell had already helped New York beat the Miami Heat, the Atlanta Hawks, and the Indiana Pacers. And in this game, he had already scored a career high 35 points. Latrell Sprewell was the Knicks' best chance of staying alive in the NBA Finals.

The ball was inbounded to Sprewell. Two giant San Antonio defenders quickly closed in. One was Tim Duncan, who stood seven feet tall. The other was David Robinson, who was seven feet one inch tall. Sprewell had to put up a quick shot over both men. The ball bounced off the rim and did not go in the basket. San Antonio was the 1999 NBA Champion.

"Their size was the ultimate difference," Sprewell said after the loss. He did not have to talk about why the Knicks had lost. He did not need to explain why he had missed that last shot. The Knicks lost the championship. To their fans, though, they were still winners.

Latrell Sprewell flies through the air past his defender.

Latrell Sprewell was a winner, too. Knick fans now call out his name at home games. During the 1998–99 season, Latrell Sprewell found a home with the Knicks.

A Born Winner

"I have a drive that I don't know if every player has," Latrell Sprewell once said. "I'm a guy that wants to win at everything I do, whether it's video games or basketball. You name it. I want to win at it."

Latrell Fontaine Sprewell was born on September 8, 1970, in Milwaukee, Wisconsin. Growing up, he learned to be a respectful, polite young man. He also was very close to his family. Today, Latrell Sprewell says the people he most admires are his parents and his grandparents.

While he was growing up in Wisconsin, young Latrell liked sports. But he did not know much about basketball. He lived in the home city of the NBA's Milwaukee Bucks. But he was not a Bucks fan. He grew up rooting for the Dallas Cowboys of the National Football League (NFL). He loved the Cowboys. As a boy, he dreamed of someday playing wide receiver for Dallas. Latrell Sprewell did not play basketball in elementary school or middle school. He did not play varsity basketball until his last year of high school. During his last year of high school, he finally started playing the game that he would grow to love.

Latrell used the same winning feelings in his everyday life that he used on the basketball court. He began to show everyone he could really play. He averaged 28 points per game in his final year at Washington High School.

Unfortunately, he was not noticed by college scouts. (College scouts watch the better players in high schools to see who they might want to play for their college team.) Playing only one year of varsity basketball had hurt his chances. Now he probably would not win a scholarship to play at a top college.

★★★ UP CLOSE

Latrell Sprewell enjoys playing with computers and videos. He used to work out the bugs in video games that his brother created. Another of his favorite things to do is fixing stereos.

Latrell Sprewell did not play basketball until his last year of high school. He began to show everyone he could really play.

Winning a scholarship is one way to help pay the cost of a college education. Latrell Sprewell would first have to show he was ready and willing to be an even better player.

CHAPTER

3

The Big Time

For Latrell Sprewell success in basketball was not quick or easy. He graduated from high school. Then he went to Three Rivers Community College in Missouri. He worked hard to become a better basketball player. During his second year of college, Sprewell began to really stand out on the basketball court. He led his team to a great 32–8 record.

Sprewell led the team on defense and offense. He had 9.2 rebounds per game and scored 26.6 points per game. He set a single season school record for most points scored. In just two years, Sprewell scored the most career points ever by a player at Three Rivers Community College.

College coaches began to notice Sprewell. He got a scholarship to play

★★★ **UP CLOSE**
★

At the University of Alabama, Latrell Sprewell studied social work. That means he learned how to help people. In 2000, he gave $100,000 to Madison Square Garden's Cheering for Children Program. The money was used to buy sports equipment for children.

Latrell Sprewell reaches above the other players to get the ball.

basketball at the University of Alabama. In Alabama, Sprewell played with Robert Horry. Horry would later play for the Houston Rockets and the Los Angeles Lakers in the NBA.

In Alabama, Sprewell became known as a player who was very good both on defense and on offense. The 1990–91 season was his first year at Alabama. He started 17 of 33 games. He also averaged 8.9 points per game, and his shooting percentage was .535.

In his last year at Alabama, Sprewell led the Southeastern Conference (SEC) in minutes played. He averaged 36.2 minutes per game. He also averaged 17.8 points and 5.2 rebounds per game.

In 1991–92, Latrell Sprewell was voted to the All-Southeastern Conference First Team. He was also named to the All-SEC Defensive Team. The next stop for Latrell Sprewell was the NBA.

Boo! Boo! Boo! Fans of the Golden State Warriors loudly protested their team's first choice in the 1992 NBA Draft. The draft is the way that teams choose new players each year. The Warriors had made Alabama's Latrell Sprewell their first pick. The fans wanted a big man who could play center or power forward. They did not want Latrell Sprewell.

But the boos quickly turned to cheers when Sprewell began playing for Golden State. He amazed fans with his energetic style of play.

"When you're watching Latrell, it's like watching a video game," explained Marcus Camby of the New York Knicks. "You can hear the sound effects!"

Latrell Sprewell averaged 15.4 points per game during his first season in the NBA in 1992–93. He also had 126 steals, 295 assists, and 52 blocked shots. He pulled down 271 rebounds. Latrell Sprewell became the first Golden State player in history to score more than 1,000 points in his first year. He had 1,182 points total.

Sprewell was rewarded for his efforts. He was named to the All-NBA Rookie Second Team. He also got the Jack McMahon Award. This was voted on by his teammates. It meant he was Golden State's Most Inspirational Player.

In his second NBA season, Sprewell got even better. He led Golden State in scoring with an average of 21 points per game. He took the place of the recently retired Michael Jordan on the All-NBA First Team. Sprewell was only twenty-three. He also became the youngest guard ever named to the NBA's All-Defensive Team. The future looked bright for Latrell Sprewell. He was proving himself on the court. Teammate Chris

★★★ UP CLOSE

Latrell Sprewell was very sad when the Golden State Warriors traded away his friend Chris Webber. He wore Webber's number on the back of his basketball shoes as a way to remember his friend.

Webber had become a good friend.

Then trouble began. The Golden State Warriors traded away Chris Webber. Sprewell felt the team had let a key player go.

After Webber left, Sprewell still played very well. But Golden State began to crumble as a team. The losses added up.

"When I was at Golden State I didn't have the type of team where I could realistically say I was going to get to the NBA Finals," Sprewell admitted

In only his second NBA season, Latrell Sprewell was leading the Golden State Warriors in scoring.

Latrell Sprewell flies to the basket.

in 2001. Latrell Sprewell liked to win at everything. He wanted an NBA Championship more than anything.

In 1996–97, Latrell Sprewell had his best season as a Warrior. He averaged 24.2 points per game. On December 15, 1996, the Warriors played the Washington Bullets (later called the Washington Wizards). Sprewell became the second NBA player in history to have 2 four-point plays in the same game. (Seattle's Dale Ellis was the other. He did it on January 26, 1988, against the Sacramento Kings.) Sprewell also scored a career-high 46 points. They came in a game against the Dallas Mavericks on January 21, 1997. He had a total of 1,938 points that season. This made Latrell Sprewell

★★★ **UP CLOSE**
★

Latrell Sprewell had his first career triple-double on March 28, 1997 in a game against the Phoenix Suns. A player gets a triple-double when he has ten or more in three different categories. Sprewell scored 31 points, had 11 rebounds, and 11 assists in the game.

the fifth-leading scorer in the NBA for the 1996–97 season.

Latrell Sprewell had done many good things on the basketball court. But he was still upset that the team had let his friend Chris Webber go. In 1997–98, Sprewell had a big argument with coach P. J. Carlesimo. He tried to choke the coach. Golden State let Sprewell go on December 3, 1997. There was a legal battle. Sprewell was let back on the team on March 4, 1998. But now he was thought of as a player with a bad attitude. He was not allowed to play for the rest of the season.

CHAPTER
5

A New Start

The New York Knicks traded John Starks, Chris Mills, and Terry Cummings to the Golden State Warriors on January 21, 1999. They got Latrell Sprewell from the Warriors in return. Sprewell overcame a foot injury early in the season. He went on to become a key player for the 1998–99 Knicks. The team went all the way to the playoffs.

During the 1999–2000 season, the Knicks and Latrell Sprewell again returned to the playoffs. They beat the Toronto Raptors and the Miami Heat. Then they lost to the Indiana Pacers in the Eastern Conference Finals.

Once again, Latrell Sprewell was a big part of the Knicks' success in 2000. He led New York in free throws made (344), assists (332), and steals (109). He also averaged 18.6 points and 4.3 rebounds per game.

Yet Sprewell still was not satisfied. He wanted to win it all. So did Knicks' coach Jeff Van Gundy. At the start of the 2000–01 season, Knicks center Patrick Ewing was traded to the

Latrell Sprewell was a big part of the New York Knicks' success in 2000.

Seattle Supersonics. This would give teammates Latrell Sprewell, Allan Houston, and Glen Rice more time on the floor together.

Early in the 2000–01 season, the New York Knicks were not playing well. Still, in almost every game, Sprewell or Allan Houston was the top scorer. After the team lost, 84–81 to the Miami Heat, Sprewell tried to get the team to play better.

"Yeah! We can win. There's no doubt about it! And we're gonna win. We just have to fine tune some things," Sprewell told the press.

New York won five of their next six games. After a loss to the Utah Jazz, the Knicks won four games in a row. Sprewell scored 25 points against the Washington Wizards. He had 32 points against the Chicago Bulls and 27 points against the Minnesota Timberwolves.

The win over the Timberwolves was important. It was the twenty-fifth game in row for the Knicks where the other team scored less than 100 points.

On January 7, 2001, the Knicks tied an NBA record for defense. The record had been set by the Fort Wayne (later Detroit) Pistons during the 1954–55 season.

"This is the best team I've ever been associated with in the NBA," Sprewell said after the win. "I've never been on a seven-game winning streak before so this is uncharted territory for me. It's fun!"

The New York Knicks broke the NBA record for games where the other team scored less than 100 points on January 11, 2001. Latrell Sprewell and his teammates held the Houston Rockets to only 76 points. The Rockets won the game though, 76–75.

The Knicks held the other team below 100 points for 33 games in a row. Then the streak ended. On January 23, 2001, the Milwaukee Bucks beat the Knicks.

Latrell Sprewell tries to get past his defenders.

The score was 105–91. Latrell Sprewell scored 21 points in the game. The Knicks, though, were really starting to like how it felt to win. And Latrell Sprewell was helping them.

6

Star Power

The NBA's 2000–01 All-Star team was announced at midseason. Many basketball fans and experts were surprised that Latrell Sprewell was not on the East's team. Sprewell's teammate Allan Houston was on the team. Everyone expected Sprewell to be named a substitute player. NBA coaches pick the substitute players.

Latrell Sprewell was not chosen by the coaches. Perhaps Sprewell's past problems with Coach Carlesimo had affected their decision. One coach did not agree with that decision. New York Knicks head coach Jeff Van Gundy said, "I was shocked that Latrell didn't make it."

Latrell Sprewell had every right to be upset. He could have complained. But he stayed calm and did not get angry. "What can you say?" Latrell told reporters. "There's not sense in getting down about it."

Grant Hill of the Orlando Magic and Alonzo Mourning of the Miami Heat could not play in the All-Star Game. They were hurt. Two

Latrell Sprewell shows his determination as he dunks the ball.

new players had to be chosen. Those players would be picked by NBA commissioner David Stern. Many people thought he too would leave Sprewell off the team. He picked two players who truly deserved to be all-stars. One was Dikembe Mutombo of the Atlanta Hawks. The other was Latrell Sprewell of the New York Knicks.

Allan Houston liked the decision. "I'm glad the League recognizes how important Spree is to our success this year because he really deserves this," he said.

Latrell Sprewell and Allan Houston helped the East All-Stars win the 2001 NBA All-Star Game.

Latrell Sprewell had already won the praise of fans. Now he was thought of as one of the league's top players by the NBA commissioner.

More to Come

Latrell Sprewell continues to prove himself on the basketball court. He has played more than five hundred NBA games in his career. He has spent some 20,000 minutes on the court as an NBA star. His total career points are already more than 10,000.

Latrell Sprewell really wants to win an NBA title. "I need that ring man," Latrell said. "I need a championship."

Businessman Latrell Sprewell owns and operates "Sprewell Racing," a high-performance tire and wheel business in San Gabriel, California.

★★ UP CLOSE
★

Famous movie maker and Knick fan Spike Lee often comes to Knick games wearing a jersey with Sprewell's No. 8 on it.

Not only does Latrell Sprewell play basketball, he also owns a business.

CAREER STATISTICS

	NBA								
Year	Team	GP	FG%	Reb.	Ast.	Stl.	Blk.	Pts.	PPG
1992–93	Golden State	77	.464	271	295	126	52	1,182	15.4
1993–94	Golden State	82	.433	401	385	180	76	1,720	21.0
1994–95	Golden State	69	.418	256	279	112	46	1,420	20.6
1995–96	Golden State	78	.428	380	328	127	45	1,473	18.9
1996–97	Golden State	80	.449	366	507	132	45	1,938	24.2
1997–98	Golden State	14	.397	51	68	19	5	299	21.4
1998–99	New York	37	.415	156	91	46	2	606	16.4
1999–2000	New York	82	.435	349	332	109	22	1,524	18.6
2000–2001	New York	77	.430	347	269	106	28	1,364	17.7
Totals		596	.434	2,577	2,554	957	321	11,526	19.3

GP—Games Played Ast.—Assists Pts.—Points Scored
FG%—Field Goal Percentage Stl.—Steals PPG—Points per Game
Reb.—Rebounds Blk.—Blocked Shots

Latrell Sprewell is
known as "Spree"
to his teammates.

Where to Write

Mr. Latrell Sprewell
New York Knickerbockers
Madison Square Garden
Two Pennsylvania Plaza
New York, New York 10121-0091

Latrell Sprewell dribbles
down court.

WORDS TO KNOW

assist—To make a pass to a player that ends in a score.

center—The player who positions himself in the middle of the floor near the basket. He is usually a team's tallest player.

foul shot—A free try at the basket after a player has been fouled. The ball is shot from the foul line.

guard—A player who plays in the backcourt. He needs to be a good dribbler and passer.

jump shot—A shot taken while leaping toward the basket.

point guard—A player who plays in the backcourt. He is a good ballhandler and is expected to run a team's offense.

power forward—A player who plays in the frontcourt. It is usually played by a team's strongest (though not necessarily the tallest) player. He must also be a good rebounder.

rebound—Getting the ball after a missed shot.

steal—To take the ball away from a player on the other team.

trade—Giving a player or players from one team to a new team in exchange for some other player or players.

triple-double—Ten or more in three categories such as scoring, rebounding, and assists.

READING ABOUT

Books

Gutman, Bill. *The Kids' World Almanac of Basketball.* Chicago, Ill.: World Almanac Books. Funk & Wagnalls, 1995.

Italia, Bob. *The Golden State Warriors.* Minneapolis, Minn.: ABDO Publishing Company, 1997.

Internet Addresses

Latrell Sprewell Player Profile
<www.nba.com/playerfile/latrell_sprewell/index.html>

Official Web Site of the New York Knicks
<http://www.nba.com/knicks>

INDEX